Mis(très)s Entrepreneur Manifesto

Edge. Torque. Integrity. Command.

Paul Lange

Manolutions Publishing

First Edition 2025
Copyright © 2025 by Paul Lange
All rights reserved.

No portion of this book may be reproduced in any form or by any means
without written permission from the publisher or author.

Contents

1. INTRODUCTION — 1
2. THIS IS NOT A SAFE SPACE — 5
3. LEADERSHIP LIES — 9
4. WHAT WE BELIEVE — 15
5. YOU'RE NOT NEW. YOU'RE DONE PLAYING SMALL. — 19
6. WHAT WE ACCEPT. WHAT WE REFUSE. WHAT MAKES 'ME' DIFFERENT. — 23
7. WHAT WE EXPECT OF YOU — 29
8. WE LEAD WHAT WE'VE LIVED — 33
9. ABOUT THE AUTHOR — 35

Chapter 1
INTRODUCTION

If you're still waiting for permission, close this now.

I built this because I was done watching brilliant people burn out while hiding who they really are, and then finding myself at the edge of the crevasse, unanchored above the abyss, one slip away from spiralling into the exact same pattern.

Not just fatigue—dissociation.
Not just exhaustion—erasure.
I saw the warning signs. This is my refusal to ignore them.

Because real leadership isn't taught.
It's remembered.
And most have forgotten.

I built this to remind myself what it looks like when you hold power deliberately. In moments when I forget my edge, this is the steel I sharpen against.

Because power, passion and precision are integral to our human experience. Too many of us shy away from what we're really good at.

Mis(très)s Entrepreneur draws on real-life work I have done with real-world Dominatrixes at the top of their game.

When I first started working with ProDommes, I assumed the business would be built on staged performance ... theatre, novelty, taboo. I was wrong. What I found instead were some of the most methodical, commercially precise operators I'd ever encountered.

They understood margins, frame control, human psychology, and client retention better than most founders and CEOs I worked with—before they got their shit together.

They didn't hustle curbside for scraps.
They moved with precision—from director suites to designer dungeons.

Their power didn't come from sex. It came from sovereignty.
They never crossed that line. They didn't need to.

They didn't run sideshows. They ran empires.
Built quietly. Scaled selectively.
And sustained longer than most C-suite players

They weren't successful because they beat people.
They were successful because they never beat themselves.

These weren't super-humans, super-heroes, Goddesses from Olympus or any other deity, but the people they served worshipped their leadership, and business profits followed arm-in-arm with *la dolce vita*.

Mis(très)s Entrepreneur is for men and women with the cojones to be unapologetically who they are. The dress-rehearsal was in the womb and it ended the moment you entered the room. Now strip back every excuse, stand naked and let the world meet what's underneath.

We're building a new class of leaders who will never apologise for commanding outcomes. When staying where you are is bleeding you six figures a year in wasted time, emotional bandwidth, and false starts, what are you going to do about it?

This is where ME begins.

Chapter 2
THIS IS NOT A SAFE SPACE

It's a return to power.

And I will not be commanded,
And I will not be controlled
And I will not let my future go on,
without the help of my soul.

- Greg Holden, 'The Lost Boy'

The life and actions of Mis(très)s Entrepreneur are not ones of oppression or abuse. They are forged in power, fuelled by pleasure, and obsessed with passion. They are a call to action to be the best you can become.

"ad majora natus"
(born for greater things)

This was branded into me before I could spell it. And I've spent more than 50 years watching people run from it or rise into it.

Realise that we were all born for greater things, greater than the majority are being or ever become, and you will be driven to select, collect, and accept everything you're currently leaving on the table.

Mis(très)s Entrepreneur is about how you show up in your own business, on your professional path, and in your personal life. Do you choose to live life on your terms or acquiesce and serve at the behest of others? Do you contribute and leave more than when you arrived or do you just consume and deplete resources?

Do you choose to lead?
Or decide that the leadership title is enough?

Mis(très)s Entrepreneur is not for everyone.
It's definitely not another coaching program.
Shakespeare summed up most coaches, consultants and trainers 420 years ago—long before LinkedIn gave them microphones.

> *"If to do were as easy as to know what were good to do, chapels had been churches, and poor men's cottages princes' palaces.*
> *It is a good divine that follows his own instructions:*
> *I can easier teach twenty what were good to be done,*
> *than be one of the twenty to follow mine own teaching."*

The industry is stacked to the rafters with people like this.

Will you be commanded?
Will you be muted?
Will you be controlled?
Will you be moulded?
Will you be marked by the crowd, hiding in the shadows of mediocrity?
Will you obey the noise?

Or honour the call, rise—and command?
And Lead.
The choice is yours. Your future is waiting.

That's a lot of questions. Only you have the answers. Mis(très)s Entrepreneur is a pathway for those willing to make choices and be accountable.

All men are created equal.
Power is a choice.
With choice comes consequence.

All men are endowed by their Creator with certain unalienable Rights.
Besides Life, Liberty and the Pursuit of Happiness,
Pleasure is your Right.

Whips, chains and canes optional.

Chapter 3
LEADERSHIP LIES

Leadership today isn't broken because people are weak.
It's broken because people have been lied to …
and they bought it.

We've been sold a script.
One polished, pleasant, and perfectly useless.

It says:

>Be empathetic.
>Be vulnerable.
>Be visible.
>But don't be too much.
>Don't go too fast.
>Don't speak too sharply.
>Don't lead too strongly.

It's a script that trains you to ask before acting.
To seek consensus before clarity.
To soften your stance until your spine is gone.

So who lied?

You don't need to pull back the curtain to know who the wizard is.
You already know.
The curtain's just there to make you feel like you don't.
The theatre's part of the illusion.
Every believable lie carries just enough truth to anchor it.
So here's the part truth—
The system is the lie.

Old-school sales never taught people to lie;
it taught them the lie—the pre-boxed pitch, the "premium" leads, the cadence that closes.

New leaders get the same treatment:
a boiler-room playbook
dressed up as a leadership programme,
wrapped in lanyards and leadership lingo.

It's like watching *Glengarry Glen Ross: Leadership Edition.*

Fresh-faced recruits are handed scripts, "leads," and quotas—
Boiler-room tactics in a boardroom suit.
They don't learn honesty vs deceit;
they learn the packaged deception, then call it leadership.

The boiler room didn't break leadership.
It just showed us what the boardroom looked like without a suit.

We've been taught to *perform leadership* from someone else's script, not *practice it* with conviction.
To posture instead of own.
To schedule instead of choose.
To quote playbooks instead of write our own.
It's bullshit instead of brilliance.

The result:
Indecision gets masked as movement, and dressed up as strategy.

We made visibility a virtue.
We made optics an orgy.
We made busyness a badge of honour.
And confusion a leadership style.

They told you:
Don't build what no one wants. Ask your market. Serve the demand.

But most people don't know what they want.
They imitate.
They follow.

La Rochefoucauld warned us: *"Nothing is so infectious as example."*
Girard showed us: *Desire is copied, not born.*
Jobs confirmed it: *"A lot of times, people don't know what they want until you show it to them."*

If you wouldn't use it yourself—don't build it.
If you wouldn't stake your name, team, and capital on it—don't sell it.
If you're just asking instead of leading—you're already lost.

Here's what they won't tell you at the leadership and management coaching summit:

- **Busyness ≠ Importance**

- **Consensus ≠ Wisdom**

- **Noise ≠ Momentum**

- **Title ≠ Traction**

And the deadliest one:

Leadership is not a promotion.

It's a debt.
A weight.
A fire.
An accountability.

You don't rise into it.
You kneel under it—and then you choose to stand anyway.
You command. Then you demand.
Not wish—demand.
Wie 'ne Knarre vorm Gesicht.

> *Du mußt nicht wünschen*
> *Du muß fordern!*
> *– wie 'ne Knarre vorm Gesicht*
> *Vergiß es, leise anzufragen*
> *Wo es langgeht*
> *Sollst du selber sagen*
>
> — Udo Lindenberg, "Gustav"

Leadership means owning the outcome—even when it hurts.
It means choosing when others hesitate.
It means speaking when others stay silent.
And doing the thing that needs doing—especially when no one else will.

It's not about being followed.
It's about being accountable when no one else wants to be.

Most so-called leaders today?
They're performing safety drills in burning buildings.
Meanwhile, real leaders are outside pouring concrete.

Mis(très)s Entrepreneur doesn't perform.
She commands.
She builds.

She bleeds for what matters.
She makes choices others are too politically polished to own.
And she does it without apologising for being the one who sees what needs to be done.

This isn't about fixing leadership.
It's about reclaiming it.

Because when power is no longer a dirty word,
leadership finally begins.

Chapter 4
WHAT WE BELIEVE

The 6Ps Code

We believe every business is a mirror.
And what it reflects is the character of its operator.

We believe passion without profit is burnout,
profit without purpose is extraction,
purpose without pleasure is martyrdom,
pleasure without planet is destruction,
planet without people is extinction,
and people without passion are rehearsing death.

> **Passion. Pleasure. Purpose. People. Planet. Profits.**
> Not a menu. A metabolic code.
> Break one, and the whole system bleeds.

The old Triple Bottom Line model wasn't wrong.
Just incomplete ...
and hijacked by ESG decks,
UN SDG scorecards,
and DEI tokens.

These monogram movements became side rooms in the optics orgy—
Environmental exaggeration.
Virtue voyeurism.
Ideological indoctrination.

Everyone watching. No one building.
Focused on appearances instead of alignment.

It's created executive erectile dysfunction.
Leaders can't move. Potential's been neutered.
Optics instead of operations.

We believe real leadership is internal first.
That's why we optimise the operator—not just the output.

So we build from the inside out:
Passion. Pleasure. Purpose. People. Planet. Profits.

6Ps not 3Ps.
Not departments. Not initiatives.
A living system—for leaders who know they were born for greater things.

You will never outgrow your self-image.
Your business won't either.
Its internal image defines its external limits.

Passion ignites.
Not what you "like." What you'd *bleed for*.

You don't scale resentment. You scale resonance.
And if you're scaling someone else's dream?
You already feel it in your nervous system.

Pleasure sustains.
Without it, systems rot.
With it, they regenerate.
Pleasure isn't a reward.
It's your operating standard.

Purpose sharpens.
It's not found on a retreat.
It's declared. Defended.
And enforced like a boundary.
No purpose? No **permission**.

People amplify.
Your ceiling is set by who you allow in the room.
Every surge is a coalition. Every collapse is a compromise.
Right people matter.
Put them in position so they can shine.

Planet contextualises.
This isn't eco-theatre. This is consequence awareness.
Every brand leaves residue.
Leave it better than you found it.

Profits validate and expand.
They're not the goal—they're the scoreboard.
Surplus is sovereignty.
No profit? No **permission to scale.**
Fake profit? Just debt in makeup.

These are not just values.
They're energetic functions.

When aligned, the 6Ps generate a circuit that feeds itself:

> **Passion sparks**
> **Pleasure sustains**
> **Purpose directs**
> **People scale**
> **Planet steadies**
> **Profits compound**

That's the circuit.
That's the code of the Mis(très)s Entrepreneur.

You don't need a slide deck.
You need rhythm. Discipline. Alignment.

Command it ... or be commanded.

Chapter 5

YOU'RE NOT NEW. YOU'RE DONE PLAYING SMALL.

This isn't for beginners.
It's for the ones who've already bled for their business.
Who've led teams, closed deals, and hit numbers—
and still wonder why it doesn't feel like enough.

It's for the operators who carry the whole damn weight—
without needing applause,
but starting to resent the silence.

This is for **the woman** who knows her presence changes rooms—
but somewhere along the way, started asking for permission again.

For **the man** who's spent years making it work for everyone else—
and now stares at his calendar like it's a prison sentence.

It's for the operators other operators call when it breaks—
the ones who fix the business, restructure the team.

The ones who steady the P&L, clean the systems,
build the wins, then step out of frame—
and still lie awake at 2am wondering if they're the joke no one's told.

Whether you were built in boardrooms, broke yourself in middle
management, or led from the shadows—I've been you.

You're not failing.
You're outgrowing your own containment.

You're not looking for inspiration.
You're looking for precision.
Structure. Alignment.
Fire that doesn't burn you out.

You're done being a genius in conflict.
Done leaking power
to people who don't deserve your attention.
Done waiting for permission
from systems you know are broken.

You don't need help starting.
You need power re-routed.
Fast. Clean. Aligned with who you've always been before you forgot.

Mis(très)s Entrepreneur is not for the aspiring.
It's for the initiated.
The burnt-out badass.
The closeted visionary.
The man who's mastered the metrics but lost the mission.
The woman who can lead ten departments
but hasn't heard her own voice in years.

MIS(TRÈS)S ENTREPRENEUR MANIFESTO

If you're not ready, that's fine.
But if you felt this in your gut—
you weren't built to play small,
nor were you meant to be manageable.
You were built to choose. Start acting like it.

Because let's be honest
if you were meant to be controlled you would have come with a remote.
You didn't read this to be reminded.
You read it to remember.

Chapter 6

WHAT WE ACCEPT. WHAT WE REFUSE. WHAT MAKES 'ME' DIFFERENT.

You've done the polite version.
You've done the performance.
The corporate theatre.
The offsite with the agenda decks, trust falls,
laminated values and team selfies.

You've been told leadership means listening more, softening edges, holding space, lowering your voice.

We're done with that.

You've been told to lead for others.
You've carried teams, cultures, and visions that weren't yours.
You've been "we" for too long.

This is where ME returns.

Mis(très)s Entrepreneur isn't a title.
It's a sovereign system.
A recalibration.
A remembering.
A structure for those who forgot their own edge.

You'll know when ME is online—
because compromise becomes intolerable.

They say there's no "I" in team.
Hell, you've probably parroted it yourself.

But look closer.
In block letters, the "I" hides in plain sight, in the space created by A.

Strip out the noise, and all that's left is: I AM.

Strong leaders will look at TEAM and know ME was always there.
That I AM was the strength and the reason anything ever moved.

> Thirty spokes share the wheel's hub;
> It is the center hole that makes it useful.
> Shape clay into a vessel;
> It is the space within that makes it useful.
> Cut doors and windows for a room;
> It is the holes which make it useful.
> Therefore profit comes from what is there;
> Usefulness from what is not there.
>
> —*Laozi, Tao Te Ching*

Leadership is not earned by dilution.
You can keep balance.
I'll take brilliance in harmony—everytime.
Safety is not a virtue—it's a sedative. Conviction is the cure.

This is not a safe space.
It's a structured one.
And structure, by nature, creates friction.
Friction reveals alignment.
Alignment generates power.

We don't hold space.
We hold the line.

We don't facilitate "safe processing."
We facilitate sovereign choices.

We don't teach vulnerability as currency.
We treat power as precision.

The dominatrix isn't a metaphor. She's a model.
Not for theatre. Not for titillation.
Forged in real life, real relationships, and real business.
Where every gesture is intentional.
Where the paradox of control is understood, not performed.

She doesn't dominate to impose—she leads to liberate.
Because real power doesn't shout. It **holds frame.**
And real dominance doesn't strip choice. It creates space within it.

She knows you only have one life—
no matter how many roles you're asked to play.
Split identity breeds dissonance.

Sometimes it's your job.
Sometimes it's your home.
Sometimes it's both.
But the outcome is always the same:
Chaos, uncontained—the **excrement of chaos.**
Not the elegant symmetry of chaos theory—just its mess.

You weren't designed to divide.
You were built to cohere.
Integration isn't indulgence.
It's power—aligned.

You don't need a work self and a home self.
You need one self—aligned.

The women I knew didn't lead through chaos.
They ruled it—through **frame.**
Structure.
Deliberate constraint.
Voluntary tension.

She doesn't make it safe.
She makes it sovereign.
Starting with herself.

That's not therapy. That's architecture.

We don't coach mindset.
We recalibrate operators.
We strip back layers that were never yours.
We remove permission-seeking from your muscle memory.
We name what's working—and demand more of it.
We name what's not—and cut it.

You don't need more input.
You're starved for signal.

We don't believe you need to be softened.
We believe you need to realign.

You don't need another model.
You need a mirror you can't look away from.

If it doesn't challenge you, it isn't leadership.

Safe leadership is forgettable.
It's theatre.
It's the plague that passes for culture.
Aligned leadership echoes.
It's remembered in clarity.

This isn't reinvention.
This is Exodus—of the false, the flat, the filtered.
There is no better person for you to be than ME.

It doesn't require explanation. Just ownership.
I no longer belong to that script.
I belong to ME.

Say it.
I AM. ME.

The Operator's Dilemma

To be ME, or not to be ME—that is the question.
Whether it's safer to suffer
the meetings, the metrics, the models,
the middle-managers, the mediocrity
or to Exodus the corporate conditioning,
and by rebellion—end it.

We've survived the plagues.
Now we exit the scripts.
I AM ME. I AM Mis(très)s Entrepreneur.

Chapter 7
WHAT WE EXPECT OF YOU

Only Co-Conspirators Admitted. Step In or Step Out.

This is a pact.
You're here to be held to a standard most people can't stomach.

No sign up. No sandbox.
You show up and step in—fully.
Energetically present. Emotionally available. Strategically sharp.

You don't come here to be handheld.
You come here to be challenged—as a peer.
No mutual masturbation-fest.
No mentor-as-therapist dynamics.

Instead—Mutual ignition. Combustion. Thrust.

The truth is, you've already led.
Already built.
Already carried more weight than most people recognise.

But now you're bleeding energy through indecision, distraction, dilution.
That's not failure.
That's misalignment.

You don't come here to be guided.
You come here to be held to the fire of what you already know.
Because you've already been the smartest person in too many rooms.
That's not the flex you think it is.
It's the weight that's crushing your breath and leaking your bandwidth.

We won't coddle it.
We'll name it.

We won't fix it for you.
We'll expose it with you.

We match energy.
We hold a mirror to misalignment.

No spectators. No consumers.
You're here to calibrate. Contribute. Co-create.

Bring presence. Participate.
You don't access the work—you become it.
Power doesn't respond to spectators.

The moment you default to "client" thinking—you've missed the point.
This isn't client work. This is operator work.
Peer work—not therapy.
Not coaching. Not command-and-control.
If you need emergency rescue—call 911/000.
This is not a hotline. This is a sovereign signal.
Kings talk to Kings!

MIS(TRÈS)S ENTREPRENEUR MANIFESTO

Here's what we expect:

- **Declare or disappear.**
  If you can't name what you want
  you'll burn everyone's time—including yours.
  Without a destination no one can help you move.

- **Drop the costume.**
  No curated story. No humblebrag.
  No achievement cosplay. No edge-softening for optics.
  This isn't LinkedIn. This is a leadership crucible.
  Come naked—or don't come.

- **Hold frame.**
  Especially when it shakes.
  The room doesn't bend around your discomfort.
  You bend around your commitment—or you break.
  We don't do reparenting.
  Hold the frame—or get out of it.

- **You stay in the room.**
  Especially when it stings.
  Especially when you want to run.
  The edge you avoid is the edge that defines your next level.

We don't expect perfection.
We expect **presence**.

We don't expect certainty.
We expect **clarity in motion.**

We don't expect obedience.
We expect **ownership**.

This isn't about being teachable.
It's about being **reachable**.
Energetically. Intellectually. Relationally.

You don't get a gold star for showing up.
You get a mirror—and the choice to keep looking.

We don't care how successful you are.
We care how honest you are.
Because skill without sovereignty is still slavery.
You've done performative leadership.
You've survived corporate etiquette.
You've mastered optics.

This is the cost of truth.
Pay it, or pass.

We're not here to manage your energy.
We're here to match it. Multiply it. Mirror it.

We're not for everyone.
We're not for most.

If that stings, pause. Don't run.
The work begins where the flinch ends.

This isn't personal development.
It's personal dominion.
It's where ME leads.

And if that hits—we're already building.

Chapter 8

WE LEAD WHAT WE'VE LIVED

We've done it wrong, and learned the lessons.
We've paid the price, but refused to be bankrupted.

We reject victimhood.
We are Invictus—unbroken by a stacked system.

That's why we built this—not for followers,
but for those prepared to stand on the wall and command.

Master of our fate. Captain of our soul.
We lead what we've lived.

Out of the night that covers me,
Black as the pit from pole to pole,
I thank whatever gods may be
For my unconquerable soul.

In the fell clutch of circumstance
I have not winced nor cried aloud.
Under the bludgeonings of chance
My head is bloody, but unbowed.

Beyond this place of wrath and tears
Looms but the Horror of the shade,
And yet the menace of the years
Finds and shall find me unafraid.

It matters not how strait the gate,
How charged with punishments the scroll,
I am the master of my fate,
I am the captain of my soul.

Invictus—William Ernest Henley

Chapter 9
ABOUT THE AUTHOR

Paul Lange doesn't care for titles or political correctness.
He calls bullshit when he sees it.
Here's what else you should know.

He's already spent 35+ years in the game—launching, scaling, and exiting businesses across hospitality, private equity, and advisory.

He doesn't advise from the balcony.
He builds in the bloodshed.

He's coached executives and founders alike who wear masks, walking around with their eyes wide shut, and helped them strip down to something real.

Rulers on paper. Submissive in practice.
They led org charts. But obeyed expectations.
Leadership is happening either way—the only question is, who's in control?

He believes business is neither theatre nor therapy and that domination, in commerce, starts with self-command, not conquest.

He once got asked if he was a priest, a drug dealer, or a hitman.
He said yes.

The architect of Total QX (Total Quality Experience) and author of "The 20% Leader" and "Evolve or Be Remembered", Paul works with executives and founders who want to ditch the role-play for reality, with no room for self-delusion. They've outgrown the applause and are ready to lead with power and precision.

This manifesto exists because executives and founders have surrendered their sovereignty, are being weighed down by wokeness, dominated by DEI and are ejaculating ESG. They've forgotten who holds the leash—the business, or them. And now they whimper when it pulls. If this leaves you uncomfortable, good. It's not here to entertain. It's here to wake the operator up. Read it if you want. Act on it if you're ready.

www.ingramcontent.com/pod-product-compliance
Lightning Source LLC
Chambersburg PA
CBHW061235070526
44584CB00030B/4134